EMPATH AND PSYCHIC ABILITIES

Learn How to Develop Your Psychic Abilities with Guided Meditations and How to Thrive as an Empath

Table of Contents

Introduction

Psychics and empaths do have some crossover, but contrary to popular belief, they are not the same, which is why it is essential to define what it means to be a psychic, an empath, and a psychic empath. Once you understand the key differences and similarities, you can begin training your psychic empath skills.

Psychics and Their Powers

While the media often sensationalizes psychics and their gifts, psychic powers and aptitude are both common. Psychics have extrasensory perceptions (ESP) that they can use to obtain information beyond what can be sensed by ordinary perceptions. They can use their minds to look beyond the physical world's sensations and gather information from more spiritual realms. For example, if you look outside, you will see that the grass is green, but psychics can see beyond the concreteness of the physical world, and they can become more aware of what they can sense that is not surface level.

Among psychics, there are several methods of tapping into extra sense and learning about the future, the past or communicating with the dead—among other skills. They have unique gifts that allow them to see beyond the physical world. Each psychic will have different aptitudes, and you need to become aware of what your skills are and what methods you are drawn to, which you will explore throughout this book in detail. Of course, while there is some degree to which your skills are inherent in you, skills can be magnified and improved upon if you put them to work. So even if you don't feel particularly psychic, don't get discouraged. There is hope for you to get in touch with sensations that you never paid attention to before. The more you experiment with your ESP, the better relationship you will have with your psychic empathy.

Many people believe that psychics aren't real, and some of the psychics you see on TV shows and in stage performances may be charlatans. These practitioners should not be mistaken for genuine psychics because they generally use the normal senses to make guesses and reach likely conclusions based on what they sense. Real psychics may not have as much glitz and sensationalism, but they can reach new planes with their senses, and while they may not always have complete reads, they will often have inexplicable intuition that comes from their ESP. Charlatans often give all psychics a bad reputation, making it hard for people to understand their psychic gifts and how to utilize them best.

Otherworldly experiences are often discouraged and treated as superstitious. This attitude closes us off from our psychic skills, making it harder to be taken seriously on our metaphysical journey. Thus, people who develop psychic gifts as children often stifle their abilities and suppress their sensations. As a result, they remain somewhat intuitive and empathetic, dismissing their extrasensory information rather than embracing it. Society makes it seem like psychics are weird or liars, but that is so far from the truth, and you need to erase that line of thought from your subconscious and conscious levels of your brain. Instead, embrace the wonders of your senses and the skills that are waiting to be reawakened within you.

Psychics are not just fakers. They truly experience the world in unique ways and have senses that allow them to know what the untrained person cannot. While psychic abilities vary, most people have some degree of skill if they channel and build that skill.

Empaths

Empaths, particularly psychic empaths, are people who will intensely sense the emotions of other people or beings near them, and they will sometimes feel these emotions even more profoundly than their feelings. They are extra sensitive to the senses and dispositions of the people around them, which makes them more aware of the suffering and joy of others. This gift can be painful, but it can also be incredibly rewarding because it facilitates a deeper connection with other people and other parts of the universe.

Most people, even non-psychic ones, will feel empathy to some extent, which is the feeling of understanding the pain (or other emotions) of someone else without necessarily having experienced that same situation yourself. It is being able to deeply thrust yourself into someone else's position and become connected to them. Empathy is unique from sympathy. Empathetic people can envision themselves in the same conditions as the people around them, and they can understand that person's perspective. It is about putting yourself in someone else's shoes and sensing their emotions. Empathy is more connective, while sympathy is more distant. Sympathy doesn't require you to understand someone else's perspective; instead, it merely understands people's feelings without experiencing them. People with empathy can go far beyond mere sympathy, and they can let themselves into people's endeavors with pain, joy, or any other emotion. Psychic empaths have a special relationship with empathy in ways that ordinary people do not.

Psychic empaths can do much more than just sense the visual or verbal cues that someone is in pain or experiencing other intense feelings. They can feel other people's emotions even when they aren't outwardly apparent, meaning that these people are extra sensitive to the feelings of others, which can make it difficult to navigate social situations and relationships without an understanding of how psychic empathy works.

There are several types of empaths, so while psychic empaths will all experience the absorption of emotional and spiritual energies around them, each person experiences these energies differently and even from various sources. An emotional empath, for example, can sense the emotional vibrations of others, while a physical empath can feel when people are physically experiencing certain sensations like pain. An intuitive empath is like an emotional one, but they see the deeper connections of the feelings beyond just the surface-level emotions. They are great at knowing when people are deceptive because of their deep intuition. Another type is a dream empath that can sense what dreams mean. They learn about others and themselves through dreams and instinctually can piece together what it all means. There are even types that don't have to do with feeling empathy for people. Plant empaths will feel empathy for plants, while animal empaths will feel empathy for animals. Similarly, earth empaths have extra sensations related to nature and can sense things like natural disasters before they occur. You may fit multiple of these categories to varying degrees, but these categories show how diverse psychic empaths are.

Empaths have a unique gift of feeling the emotions of others deeply. These skills are beautiful, and they allow people with such a gift to better their lives and deepen their connections with the non-physical world. Even if you don't think you are psychic right now, if you feel that you are an empath, you will likely build psychic skills with practice and attention to your otherworldly senses.

The Link of Psychic Skills with Empathy

Psychic skills and empathy are linked because they are both gifts that involve alignment with the universe beyond the physical. These skills allow people to use their senses to connect with the world and other people. It enables them to enter experiences with more confidence and know that they are working to be better versions of themselves. Both skills have so much overlap, even if psychic skills and empathy have unique attributes. When combined, they are incredibly powerful, which is why learning to harmonize these skills is so vital to your spiritual and emotional well-being.

Empathy is inherently otherworldly, just as being psychic is. They both connect you beyond just what is here and now, and they take you past the physical world. Both concepts show you that it pays to become more aligned with your spiritual self and listen to your gut feeling. You may doubt these feelings because of societal conditioning, but learning to live with and embrace your sensations is one of the best things that you can do to help yourself become more balanced. The physical world is excellent, but there's so much more to life that you have to address if you want to be healthy, happy, and better for the world.

Sometimes, you know that people are feeling bad, even if they act as though everything is fine. That is a sign of psychic empathy. With untrained skills, you might not pinpoint who is feeling bad, but you will feel that lousy mood instinctually because of your psychic senses. It can be confusing at first to address the feelings that seem to have no rational explanation but know that those senses are genuine. They are not physical, but that doesn't mean they are fake. The same is true of all things emotional. You cannot physically see love, but it still exists. The same is true of so many emotional aspects.

When you are empathetic, you can treat the universe and its parts with more respect and understanding. Psychic empathy enables you to see everything in whole new ways. One of the best parts of being a psychic empath is that you will start to be more respectful to everything around you because being respectful keeps harmony in the world. When there is harmony in the world, you absorb that harmony back into yourself. If you cause chaos, that chaos will then come back to you because of your empathy. Empathetic people want to do what is right and make other people feel happy because that is how they will feel ultimate happiness despite the hardships of their lives. Psychic empathy requires you to open yourself to the senses that you have rather than trying to avoid them, and in the process, you learn to be more grateful for your surroundings and for all the blessings that the universe has provided. Thus, allow your psychic and empathetic skills to work together to instill inner peace within you.

Practicing psychic empathy will help you clear the clutter in your head and live a more fulfilled life. If you avoid either the psychic or empathetic part of yourself, you deny the most genuine form of yourself. You are stifling the non-physical part of you, which always leads to discontent. You need to embrace your inner psychic empath in everything that you do. You will only ever have a balanced life if you accept who you are and your otherworldly skills. Think about your relationship with the world and your intuition and ask yourself if you have become detached from the very things that ground you and provide you with your sense of identity.

Chapter 1. Guided Meditation

General living is plagued with the existence of stress. Stress is like a pandemic because it is everywhere and affects everyone. No one is immune to stress, except the little child who is yet to know anything about life. From the time children are given homework till they graduate from school, their brains begin to adapt to the pressure to perform. As we get older, responsibilities come upon us, and we feel compelled to solve a problem staring in our face or deal with a very delicate issue. Stress is a precursor to the many illnesses we experience today.

But nature has given us a great gift called meditation that can replace some traditional medicines. When you choose to find that calm, that relief and that peace that comes from within, a portion of your brain responsible for stress control adjusts and takes in the peace you are generating at the moment. This lessens the likelihood of the onset of stress.

Stress is the body's response to an impending danger; it is triggered when the body needs to fight or flee a harmful site. When your body is stressed, all its energy is focused on getting you out of harm's way, therefore neglecting the need to have you healed from anything. A psychologist stated that pain is the source of stress and all other negative energy; when you feel pain, your body experiences stress and cannot heal the pain. Meditation takes care of the stress and calms the soul; this way, the body isn't distracted by any false alarm that triggers stress; instead, it begins to heal.

Recently, the world felt the impact of a deadly virus that left us shaking in fear and rooted in isolation. Of course, we know that isolation is usually the breeding ground for depression and anxiety. The rate at which Americans went down with depression sky-rocketed, and worse still, there was almost no means to handle the situation. Meditation is a go-to for help when you are clouded with thoughts that tend to cripple your mind.

The rate at which the world is moving is too fast for our minds to comprehend; everything seems to be in the speedy lane, leaving us in an unbalanced state. There is also the anxiety that comes due to close deadlines and huge expectations that need to be met. All this leads to a volatile mind that needs to find balance. The need to restore balance has drawn the attention of many Americans to the practice of meditation. Meditation and mindfulness help us step on the brakes and find balance.

A study was carried out on patients that had a skin disease. The patients were grouped; one group had their medications with meditation, while the other group had only medications. A few weeks later, the group that took medications with meditation sessions was four times better than the other group that took just medications.

This is very interesting but not alarming because your mind must get involved in your healing process. Interestingly, not every illness may require drugs, because working on your mind can produce the healing effect you need. The body can heal by itself through reiteration, but it won't automatically heal if it is amid factors that suppress its healing abilities. Meditation is an excellent addition to medications and can even stand on its own, but if you feel the need to add meditation to your routine drugs, by all means, do so because you will have a tremendous result. Meditation is that powerful.

Empaths are not robots; we are humans who also feel the stress and anxiety of living. We are not insulated against the psychological effects of stress, nor are we insulated from the pangs of deadlines and expectations. Thus, we need to find balance through mindful meditation practices to get grounded and find peace.

Now, don't get things mixed up; meditation does not do the healing; your body does. But your body needs meditation because it takes out the blocks from its healing path; blocks such as stressors and lack of focus hinders the body's healing abilities. So, what can meditation help you achieve health-wise? Meditation helps lower stress levels, increases focus and attention, aids in balancing thoughts, reduces the likelihood of inflammation, improves the sense of awareness, lessens pain, increases healing and repairs abilities, etc.

Studies have also proven that meditation can help lower your blood pressure, aid the body's immunity, and improve brain function. If you are constantly faced with making quick decisions, meditation can also help you get better at it because it sharpens your mind.

You've got to embrace this practice for those with mental illnesses because it will do you good. All psychologists and psychiatrists always use the meditation plan for their patients because they know its considerable benefits to the mind. So, there is a reduced likelihood of depression, anxiety, panic disorder, and even attention deficit hyperactivity disorder.

The young man had surgery and was down with pain and stress. It was so terrible that he was restless and uncomfortable. He had guided meditation for fifteen minutes, and the stress and pain went down by 60%. Meditation is indeed an answer to the prayers of most Americans.

Guided Meditation for Beginners

With all the benefits and power of meditation, it becomes fascinating to try, but you may be confused about how you can start. Meditation practice is meant to ease stress, not cause a skyrocketing of your stress levels while you are trying at it. This is the purpose of guided meditation; it shows you exactly how you should start.

- First, you need to understand some facts about meditation. Remember that like connecting with your spirit guides, you may not feel it works out immediately when you start. It's a mind thing; therefore, it is necessary to condition your mind and gradually take it through the process. Don't expect a sudden connection. You need daily meditation practice to see the manifestation of its power; a touch of consistency is advised if you need results.
- Be conscious of the place and time you choose to practice meditation. This helps eliminate distractions of every sort.
- Practice proper posture that allows you to be erect with a straight back. Also, learn and practice mindful breathing.
- A wandering mind is usual if you are just starting. So try not to be frustrated and don't judge yourself if you have a wandering mind. Don't be disappointed; it will make sense very soon if you are consistent.
- Now, think about your interests; what do you hope to achieve through meditation? Set your mind on your expectations and believe it is possible.
- Release tension from any part of your body; if you feel heavy eyes, try to close them and take cleansing breaths; if it's your chest, practice mindful breathing. The goal is to get the tension off your body.

- Try practicing the senses game; focus on each sense organ, beginning from what you see or perceive down to your feelings. This will take care of the wandering mind.
- Be sure to identify negative feelings (if you have any) and investigate the source of each one of them.

A chapter of this book is entirely made of meditation sessions of different levels to coach you in the practice. The idea of guided meditation is to have a guide walk you through the process of meditating. All you need to do is focus, stay in the present, and just flow with the vibes. Also, try to eliminate every form of distraction; this is the idea of finding a suitable place for your practice. With all the distractions gone, you can be assured of focus to a good-enough level, and soon, you will begin to see the healing power of meditation.

Chapter 2. Connecting with Spirit Guides

One aspect of meditation and spiritual work that we've touched on has been spirit guides and/or guardian angels. Spirit guides are another invaluable tool for the psychic, whether you want to meditate to simply ground yourself and replenish your energy, draw more strength to yourself before you begin a reading, or whether you seek help/protection—these are all reasons to attempt to connect with your spirit guides and ask them for advice and strength. Always treat them with respect when making requests or asking something of them. Do not demand things from them, but do not be afraid or ashamed to ask for help, as we can't do everything alone. Treat them as you would a friend or mentor.

Spirit guides or guardian angels (whichever name you use the term is clear) are not deities that you must worship; they are a spiritual presence that watches over you and guides you. You do not need to fear some godly wrath—they are on your side and want the best for you!

There are a few different types of spirit guides. Your guide may take the form of an ancestor or loved one who has passed on from the physical realm but continues to watch over you. If they are an ancestor, they may be someone who died before you were born but there are certain signs that crop up that a relative who knew them will tell you means their presence is near. For example, if you had a grandmother who loved flowers, and flowers are a constant presence in your life, this may be a sign that this ancestor is watching over you. Ancestral guides can go back many generations. You may not see the face of your ancient ancestor when connecting with them, but you will sense their relation and connection to you. You could also be watched over by a dear loved one who died during your life. This would most likely be someone who died earlier in your life as spirit guides tend to watch over you for your whole life, but it could be someone who passed on later as well.

Another common type of spirit guide is the ones that come in the form of animals. These are called "animal guides." You will likely be guided throughout your life by multiple different animal guides, each having something different to show or teach you—you won't just have one animal spirit that's assigned to you. Animal guides are often considered symbolic, or energies that embody the spirit of whichever animal it is that represents them. If you see a vision of a fierce panther while meditating, this spirit guide may offer protection and advice on assertiveness. If you see a bull calmly standing in a field, it may be there to help steady you.

Your spirit guide may not be an ancestor nor show itself as any symbolic representation. It may just be pure energy, often seen as a brilliant light. This is what many people refer to as an angel. It is likely a comforting and familiar energetic entity that has watched over you since your conception. Make sure any entity you are connecting with truly is your spirit guide. If there is any feeling of darkness or discomfort, then that entity is not your spirit guide.

Your only experience with your guide/s should be positive—that's how you know for sure.

Now that you know the basics of what a spirit guide is, let's look at how we can reach out and contact/communicate with our guides. This may be your first time interacting with your guide—you may not even know what form your guide will take yet!

Meditation is most people's go-to way to contact their spirit guide. There are many guided meditations available online for contacting your spirit guide. If you're not doing a guided meditation, when you sit down to meditate, make your only focus contacting your spirit guide. If you are contacting them for a reason, you can also focus on the reason you wish to communicate with them, but at the beginning, just focus your purpose on meeting your spirit guide. Clear your mind and don't force anything. Like with every aspect of spirituality, don't be frustrated if it doesn't work right away. Just keep sitting down to meditate with the powerful intention of contacting your spirit guide. They may not appear to you in a vision or as an image, but if you keep your mind clear and let it flow naturally, you will begin to sense their presence, and over time your communication channel with them will become stronger.

You can contact your spirit guide through meditation, but sometimes they will show themselves to you without you being in a meditative state or reaching out to them, such as a crow swooping down to stand directly in the middle of the path you were walking down, eyes fixed on you, your grandmother's scent suddenly filling your nostrils for a moment or hearing a song that you always associated with your uncle who passed away. These could all be the presence of your spirit guide.

Certain times, when your intuition strongly urges you to do or not do something, so clear it almost sounds like an inner voice is speaking to you (similar to clairaudience), this could be your guardian angel, giving advice or warnings in your day-to-day waking life. You don't have to do anything to experience this communication; just listen and acknowledge the advice. Your guide, in the spirit realm, likely knows things that you don't and has the wisdom you may not, so it's always a good idea to trust them. But at the end of the day, it's your decision to make. They are guides, not dictators.

Your spirit guide/s may visit you and show themselves to you in the form of a dream. If you've ever had a particularly vivid dream where a benign entity (whether your dead grandmother, an animal, or an energetic presence) has spoken to you, signaled to you, or led you to something/somewhere, and you remember it clearly the next day, or at least you remember the essence of what they were communicating and showing to you, this was likely a visit from a spirit guide. Though you may remember the figures you encountered and what was communicated to you when you woke up, you are likely to forget important details (if not your whole dream as the day goes by), so it's a good idea to keep a dream journal and write down exactly what you dreamed about in as much detail as you can remember after waking up. If you have to rush out the door to work, you can write in the notepad on your phone—it doesn't need to be anything fancy. If you want to keep a record of spirit guide encounters, symbolic, and important dreams, you can copy it into a paper journal when you get a chance. If you want to plan to meet a spirit guide during your dream, focus on a question you want to answer or the reason you wish to contact them before you go to sleep. As you drift into sleep with this in mind as your focus, hopefully, you will encounter them in your dream that night. This is a system of lucid dreaming, so keep in mind that it may take a few tries to have this sort of control over your dreams.

No matter what form your spirit guide takes, and what purpose they're there for, it's possible to create a strong connection and channel of communication with them through practice. Remember that if an entity that you think is your spirit guide makes you feel negatively in any way or is surrounded by any dark or unpleasant energy, that is NOT your spirit guide, and you should disconnect from them. Your interactions with spirit guides should always be positive—if somewhat introspective, or if they're a dead loved one's spirit, then possibly bittersweet. Your spirit guide and/or guardian angel only wants the best for you, and they can be a great source of support that you shouldn't hesitate to draw on.

Chapter 3. Telepathy

Telepathy is one of the most powerful psychic abilities that enables the psychic to send and receive thoughts or feelings from another person using only the power of the mind without using any physical interactions. Users of this psychic ability are often called mind readers or telepaths. Telepathy can be categorized into these two kinds: telepathic communication, which is the ability to send thoughts and feelings using the psychic's mind into another psychic's mind, and telepathic perception, which is the ability to receive thoughts and feelings using the psychic's mind from another psychic's mind. There are three major types of telepathy: instinctual telepathy, dream telepathy, and mental telepathy.

Instinctual Telepathy

Instinctual Telepathy is the type of telepathy that most of us have. It is when a psychic senses the feelings or needs of someone that is nearby via a mental connection. It uses the area around our solar plexus which is the center of our instincts and emotions. This is where the term "gut feel" came from. This type of telepathy is something that we often experience with people that we have a strong emotional and mental bond with like our loved ones such as our parents, spouse, siblings, or very close friends. The most noticeable example of instinctual telepathy involves sensing intense emotions when someone is in an emergency, serious distress, or death.

Dream Telepathy

Dream telepathy is the type of telepathy that occurs when a psychic communicates with someone's mind or receives a telepathic transmission while being in a dream. An example of this is when you have a dream about someone close to you being sad and attempting to overdose themselves with sleeping pills while in fact it is happening in real life or it is about to happen. This is a sign of telepathic transmission that you have received by having insights into that someone's mind. Another example is when you meet a friend in your dream and you tell them something, then when you wake up and meet that person in real life, you both had the same dream and they received your message. You might think that it is a coincidence, but that is a sign that you sent a telepathic transmission to your friend.

Mental Telepathy

Mental telepathy is the hardest type of telepathy to perform because it requires a lot of practice and dedication. It is the direct transmission of information from the psychic's mind to another mind. While most humans and animals have instinctual telepathy, it requires the opening of our "third eye," which opens up the mind to the world beyond our five senses. The third eye is the center of telepathy and other psychic abilities. The main difference between instinctual telepathy and mental telepathy is that instinctual telepathy occurs naturally and sometimes without even us noticing, while mental telepathy is deliberate and intentional.

How to Practice and Develop Your Telepathic Abilities

If you want to develop your telepathic abilities, it would require consistent practice and the following steps:

1. Believe in yourself and believe in telepathy

The first thing you need to do before being able to communicate telepathically is to believe in yourself that you can do it and to believe that telepathy exists. Remove all the doubts in your heart and mind and surrender yourself to the powers of your third eye.

2. Find a willing partner that you have strong bonds with

Find someone that you have strong bonds with and have an open mind who also believes in telepathy. If one of you has doubts, you may have a hard time achieving mental communication. Your partner can be a close friend, your spouse, or one of a family member.

3. Focus your thoughts

The first step to take is to calm your body and mind then focus your thoughts. Find a comfortable position and start to meditate. Tell your partner to also do the same to receive your telepathic transmission.

4. Imagine the person you are communicating with

The next thing to do while you are focused is to imagine the person you are trying to communicate with telepathically. Close your eyes and try to picture your partner and every detail about them as close as you possibly can like the way they look, how tall they are, and every specific detail that you can visualize.

5. Visualize the message you are trying to send

After imagining that the person you are trying to communicate telepathically with is in front of you, you should visualize the message you are trying to send. You can start with a simple object like a pen, try to visualize it as detailed as possible, and focus your mind only on it. Imagine the object's shape, size, color, weight, length, and all the other characteristics that you can imagine and transmit that mental image to your telepathic partner.

6. Tell the receiver to write down what came to their mind

After you have sent the telepathic message you are trying to send, your partner should remain calm and focused until they feel that the thought has entered their mind. Then you should ask them to write down what is the thought that came to their mind in complete detail. You should also write the message you are trying to send your partner.

7. Compare the results

After you both write the thought, try to compare your results and see if you both have the same things you have written down. At first, you may not be successful, but do not get discouraged because with practice you will soon be able to communicate telepathically. Just try again and practice until you can consistently tell what each other is thinking about.

How to Tell the Difference Between Telepathy and Imagination

Finding the difference between telepathy and imagination is as simple as creating an experiment with your telepathy partner. You can also confirm if your vision is telepathy or imagination by asking the people involved in your vision. For example, when you suddenly see a picture in your mind that shows your spouse in a dangerous situation. You should definitely call them immediately and ask them to confirm but do not suddenly ask them questions that will freak them out like "Did you have an accident, are you okay?" Instead, you can ask them for other specific details that can be connected with your vision like "Where are you right now?" or "What are you currently doing?" After that, you can compare their answers to see if it is connected to the vision you saw.

Do not worry, you will only be confused about it in the beginning. Once you get comfortable with your ability, you will be able to tell right away if it is just your imagination or it is a telepathic transmission.

Chapter 4. Aura Reading

One of the most hotly debated topics within the psychic community and the scientific community is that of auras. Mystics and spiritual traditions have promoted the existence of auras for millennia, covering just about every culture across the globe. Despite the widespread belief in auras, many still dismiss their existence because most people cannot see them. Recent scientific studies have revealed that auras can exist, giving credence to the ancient traditions. However, despite their findings, many scientists still debate the nature of auras and the significance they hold. Regardless of this ongoing debate, many people crave the ability to see and interpret the auras of people around them. This will provide the tools needed for seeing auras and insights regarding the true nature of auras and the meaning behind the different forms and colors they can take.

A Basic Overview of Auras

In most spiritual traditions, the nature and appearance of auras are essentially the same. A person's aura is the energy that surrounds their body, forming a sort of envelope or bubble of pulsating, glowing energy that reflects their physical, emotional, and mental state of being. Sick people, for example, will have darker, less vibrant auras, some of which even seem incomplete with holes or areas missing. In contrast, healthy, happy people will have brighter auras, usually yellow or white, extending as far as three or four feet from their body, creating a virtual bubble of energy that shields them from negative energy in their surroundings.

Although the basic elements of an aura are largely agreed upon in terms of their size, their vibrancy, and the impact of positive and negative forces upon them, there are a few debates within psychic circles regarding the meaning of their colors. Some schools of thought claim that auras can contain the same colors as chakras, meaning something similar, if not exactly the same as their chakra counterpart. However, other traditions hold that there are fewer colors and that these colors hold a completely different meaning. A perfect example is the color red. While some traditions claim that red indicates sexuality, assertiveness, and competitive nature, others suggest that it reflects anger or high levels of stress. Subsequently, context is all-important when it comes to interpreting the colors of auras as red may indicate that the individual is strong-willed or rage-driven and, thus, should be kept at a safe distance.

As already mentioned, numerous scientific studies have concluded that auras do, in fact, exist. However, these studies do little to support the idea that different colors represent different psychic abilities or spiritual qualities. Instead, the basic belief within the scientific community is that auras are nothing more than the electromagnetic field surrounding a living being. This is what is referred to as the bio-energetic field within the scientific community. The different functions of the human body, such as circulation, digestion, and respiration, all create electrical impulses that travel throughout the body. Furthermore, these impulses create electrochemical reactions throughout the nervous system. Subsequently, when a person is in peak health, where all of these functions are operating at their highest levels, a tremendous amount of electrical activity occurs all through the body, creating a halo effect around the individual. The healthier and more vibrant the individual is the brighter their bio-energetic field. When a person is ill or has suffered trauma, this field is reduced, both in size and intensity.

While science believes that an aura is largely one layer of energy produced by the electrochemical activities within the body, certain spiritual traditions believe that there are as many as seven separate layers of an aura, each representing a unique quality or condition of the individual. These seven layers of the aura are as follows:

Layer One: Etheric

This layer is the one closest to the body and is usually the easiest to see. Associated with the root chakra, it represents a person's physical health and wellbeing and is bright blue when the individual is in good health. Physically active people tend to have the brightest etheric layers.

Layer Two: Emotional

The emotional layer surrounds the etheric layer and is connected to a person's emotional wellbeing. Associated with the solar plexus chakra, it can be any color in appearance—the brighter the color, the healthier the person. When the colors are dark or muted, it represents stress, fatigue, or generally poor emotional health.

Layer Three: Mental

The mental layer is the third of the body and is associated with a person's mental health and wellbeing. It is associated with the sacral chakra—this layer is bright yellow when in good health. Due to the cognitive nature of this level, it is easiest to see around the head and neck area and is most vibrant in creative people and intellects.

Layer Four: Astral

This level is the fourth from the body and is associated with the heart chakra. Representing an individual's interpersonal relationships, it is pink or rosy red, most vibrant among those with loving personalities. In contrast, it can be subtle or even absent in introverts or those suffering heartbreak or depression.

Layer Five: Etheric Double

The etheric double layer is associated with the throat chakra and is the layer that represents your true self. This is another layer that can contain any color, depending on the qualities of the individual. When a person lives a life per their true nature, this level will be most vibrant; however, someone who is disconnected from their true identity will have a muted fifth layer.

Layer Six: Celestial

Represents unconditional love and connection with all living things; this level is pearl-white and associated with the third eye chakra. Psychics and other spiritually-minded individuals display strong celestial layers.

Layer Seven: Ketheric Template

As the last layer, this is the furthest from a person's physical body, reaching an estimated three feet. It is associated with the crown chakra; this layer is gold in color and has the highest frequency vibration. It is considered the embodiment of a person's immortal soul; thus, it reflects the individual's wellbeing across all incarnations. It also demonstrates the strength of a person's connection to the divine source.

Interpreting the Different Colors

There are two leading schools regarding the different colors of the aura and their meaning. The more common interpretation will be used for this book, specifically associated with the chakras' colors. The following are the colors of the aura and their meanings:

- **Dark red:** someone with a dark red aura will generally be hardworking, energetic, and active.
- **Bright red:** a bright red aura points to someone who has a highly competitive spirit, strives to win at whatever they do and is usually sexually assertive, harnessing raw, primal energy.
- **Orange:** a person with an orange aura is usually very business-minded, capable of handling facts and figures, and being good with people. They can also prove adventurous in nature, such as an entrepreneur.
- **Bright orange/yellow-orange:** this color points to someone with an academic nature, given logic and deep thinking.

- **Yellow:** as the color might suggest, a yellow aura represents someone bright and sunny, in disposition, spontaneous and expressive.
- **Bright green:** people with bright green auras are generally social, given community activities and occupations, such as teaching or daycare.
- **Dark green:** a dark green aura suggests someone good at organizing and being goal-oriented.
- **Blue:** this color signifies a sensitive person that is a loyal and caring friend.
- **Indigo:** a person with an indigo aura is usually more introverted, preferring solitude and tranquility. As a result, they are typically calm and clearheaded, often showing artistic qualities.
- **Violet:** a violet aura can be found in charismatic people, often with a sensual personality, and who can easily make connections with others.
- **Lavender:** highly sensitive, even to the point of being fragile; lavender aura people are very imaginative and in touch with higher levels of consciousness.
- **White:** this is the highest color, representing transcendence, spirituality, and a unity of body and mind.

One of the main things to look for, in addition to the color itself, is the brightness of the aura. When a person is healthy, happy, and in tune with their inner, true nature, their aura will be brighter and more vibrant. In contrast, someone who is depressed, ill, or suffering internal conflict will have a muted aura, sometimes even brown, representing their energy's dark, dreary condition.

Chapter 5. Intuition

Intuition can be defined as the individual's ability to have or obtain express knowledge or sudden insight without reasoning, observations, or thinking. People place a lot of premium on their gut feelings when making unfamiliar decisions. Such instinctive feelings are what intuition is all about. Your instinct guides you when going through uncertainty or charting a new course that seems to be against all available evidence.

Intuition plays a crucial role in management, sports, and entrepreneurship, where one is forced to make unclear decisions to succeed. In such situations, intuition acts as their only companion to guide the best way to act.

Clairvoyance

It means clear seeing. With this form of intuitive ability, you see things clearly in your mind as pictures, symbols, short movies, impressions, or images. Of all the 4 intuitive abilities, this is believed to be the most symbolic. Such films or pictures can be in black and white or color. Also, they can be impressions creating a vision in your mind's eye. People with intuitive clairvoyance ability often have vivid dreams, which are caused by their awakened intuition.

Clairaudience

It means clear hearing. With this intuitive ability, you hear information inside your mind. This information is received as a song lyric, sound, statement, or you may sense it as a vibration. Of all the intuitive types, it is considered the easiest because it can be heard. People with this type of ability are called clairaudients. This is because they have an area situated below the temples but above the ears, enabling them to receive such intuitive information.

Clairsentience

This is probably the most common of the 4. It is when you feel something is going to happen. If you've ever heard someone use the phrase "I can just feel it" or "this doesn't feel right," this is clairsentience. Clairsentience is often called your "gut feeling" or your instinct. Another aspect of clairsentience is being able to sense the emotions of others. Maybe you feel a wave of sadness before your friend walks into a room, and then they tell you their mother has passed away. Maybe you're on the phone with your friend who has a broken right leg, and you feel a brief pain in your right leg, even before knowing they broke it. Maybe you see your pet and suddenly burst into tears, overwhelmed by sadness for no apparent reason, and within a week, your pet dies. These are examples of clairsentience.

Claircognizance

It is when your intuition helps you figure something out that your rational brain can't, something you're maybe stuck on. For example, if you're stuck in traffic, should you risk taking the upcoming exit to get out of it and take the backroad, or will that end up taking longer? You inexplicably decide to wait it out, and soon traffic has cleared, and you're on your way. This is claircognizance. If you've ever heard someone say, "I just know," and they have no evidence to prove their certainty or no way of knowing but end up being right—that is claircognizance.

Chapter 6. How to Boost Your Psychic Ability

1. Be Willing to Use Your Psychic Abilities

Fear is one of the main factors that stop people from exploring their psychic as well as intuitive skills. People are terrified of their innate powers, but they are not dangerous. They are constantly there to guide us along the right route and serve as life's navigational instruments. Simply being ready and willing to draw into your unearthly skills is the basic step in mastering this advice. Declaring the world, you are prepared and willing to explore such abilities, and you will not be stopped by fear.

2. Practice Detecting People's Energy

Your psychic perception is coming out when you do get a terrible feeling from any person for no apparent reason, and sensing people's energy in this manner is a talent you can improve. You try to read the power of new individuals you encounter by looking over their looks and how they talk rather than tapping into their power for information. Simply being in their company may help you comprehend your own views of how your feelings affect them. This may be done without looking at it or communicating with the individual. When you are in line at a supermarket, for example, draw the power of the individual in front of you and watch what pops up. Then start up a discussion to determine which part of the knowledge your intuition picked up turned out to be accurate.

3. Make Predictions About How Locations Will Seem

A psychic ability may be used in a variety of ways, including sensing and interpreting energy. You may also work on your psychic vision, often known as clairvoyance. A remote viewing practice helps to accomplish this: Keep your eyes closed and proclaim that you desire to see this area; you are planning to visit somewhere you have never visited. Then, on a sheet of paper, sketch whatever comes to mind. Compare your image to the real appearance of the location when you arrive. You will notice that your images were already there. Sometimes, it is incredibly detailed, as you draw the same window and the identical plant in exact position.

4. Communicate with Your Guides

All humans have spirit guides to whom we may turn for help. These advanced heavenly soul mentors assist us in guiding and teaching us. Anyone we have lost who now has gone over the other side is also tied to us. Requesting a particular sign is one approach to communicate with your guides. For instance, if you desire to know whether you are on the correct track, you may ask the universe for confirmation by asking to see the purple giraffe. It is better to be very explicit in your desire for a symbol so that you can be sure that it comes from your spirit guides when you get it.

Chapter 7. Open Your Third Eye

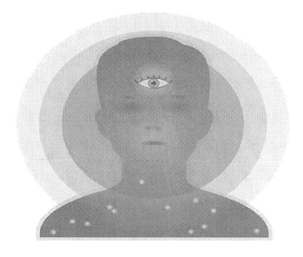

Once you have stimulated your third eye, you will be able to see how your initial decisions have influenced your life and how present decisions will affect your future. You will develop mental flexibility to see the difference between what something seems to be and what it is. With the help of your sixth chakra, you will move past normal abilities. The following strategies will help you to open your third eye chakra:

Get Grounded

The first thing you need to do before opening your third eye is to have your feet grounded. Also, it's essential to go at this slowly and create a good foundation that will give you a good amount of discernment to read your new perceptions with clarity.

Grounding is crucial because you need to have plenty of energy coursing through your energy system to support a healthy opening. Once you have activated your third eye, the information you get will likely seem unusual and possibly even disturbing. When you have enough energy and are grounded, you will expand yourself into these new perceptions. This will allow you to avoid common negative side effects of a third eye awakening, like confusion.

Create Silence

You must learn how to have silence in your mind. This can be accomplished through meditation, sitting quietly by yourself, or allowing yourself to be lost in your favorite sport or art. This helps because your third eye will bring your senses to new levels. Many people will refer to this as "space in-between" or psychic abilities. To listen to the information you send through your third eye, you have to hear a whisper. If you have a busy mind, you will likely miss your messages.

Focus on Your Intuition

There are lots of different ways to improve your intuition. Since your third eye is your center of wisdom and vision, it helps you know your dreams and what they mean. You may even want to try out lucid dreaming or try reading tarot cards. Find different ways to use your intuition during your day.

Since your third eye is where your higher perception levels live, it helps to be more tuned in with your intuition. You don't have to be perfect at intuition. All you need to do is be curious and learn more about intuitive techniques. After some practice, these techniques will become familiar, and you will be confident in your abilities. The great thing is, there's no need to be serious about it. You can have fun and explore things so that you can keep your chakras open to wonder.

Express Creativity

Allow your creativity to flow by using activities that will allow your imagination to let loose. For example, try learning something new. Don't worry about being perfect. Allow your inspiration to control your hands, and be open to whatever results you get.

Creativity is a perfect way to allow your rational mind to loosen. All of that mental chatter that tells you that something is wrong or right—and that likes to control every little thing that you do—will be silenced with creativity. When you can silence this area of your mind and use all of the available possibilities, your third eye will start to blossom.

Chanting

Chanting a mantra will help you to listen to yourself. You can repeat the seed sound for the third eye chakra, AUM, as long as you can keep your focus. You can choose some of the words that I will list below to create your mantra. Pick what works best for you. Repeat them in rhythm with your breath while meditating. You can also repeat them to yourself during the day in a Japa fashion. It should become one with your consciousness.

- SOHAMSO (soe-ha-hm-soe)
- HAMSA (ha-hm-saw)
- VIJNANA (veez-hn-ya-nah)

To help you connect even more with your third eye, you can follow these extra tips. Here are some great ways to improve your intuition and energy:

- Grow psychic awareness
- Practice contemplation
- Work with your spirit guides
- Connect with nature and the elemental energies
- Cultivate curiosity about symbols
- Focus on the space "in-between" things
- Allow your imagination freedom
- Guided meditation
- Visualization
- Dream interpretation and lucid dreaming
- Practice divination
- Strengthen your root and throat chakra
- Allow yourself to be comfortable in silence
- Mediate under the moon
- Practice intuition

The Pineal and Pituitary Glands

If you look up information about the third eye, you will likely start seeing information about the pineal and pituitary glands. Glands and chakras tend to have an intimate relationship because they all represent bodily functions. The pituitary gland is the "master gland" because it controls the majority of other glands and the production of hormones.

The pineal gland is found in the middle of your brain and is in line with your eyes. Yogic traditions see this gland as the seat of the soul and as the source of psychic abilities. The pineal gland produces melatonin and regulates our sex maturation and sleep cycle. To help awaken your third eye, you need to nurture your pineal gland. Here's how you can help your pineal gland:

- Take time in complete darkness because it will stimulate the gland and produce what is needed to correct hormones.
- Meditate because it balances the nervous system's activities and stimulates various areas of the brain.
- Take supplements and eat foods that support a healthy pineal gland like tamarind fruit, apple cider, and iodine.
- Get a lot of natural light.

Obstacles

Most people will run into some problems when trying to open their third eye. Here are some of the most common problems:

- They tend to descend consciousness, are conceited
- Their ego is attached to powers
- They communicate on the surface
- They use information about others for their gain
- They do foolish things
- They ignore what their body tells them

- They aren't dreamy
- They have self-deceiving truths
- They get distracted by details
- They listen to others through their concerns
- They see others as different
- They are rigidly rational

If you can overcome these issues and follow the techniques explained above, you will be able to open your third eye, and experience life in a new light.

How to Open Third Eye

Keeping the third eye open and energy flow as free-flowing as possible is essential to not only harness your spiritual powers but also to return safely and sanely from those realms beyond human consciousness, a common outcome of kundalini awakening. These strategies have been known to work magical wonders to open the third eye and keep its energy balanced and unblocked.

Cultivate Silence

Learn to foster the silence of your mind. For an average human, the mind is a cacophony of thoughts and ideas that threaten to take our world by storm. Not only this, but these thoughts also create a lot of noise in our minds. We can hear and interpret the messages that come to us from the higher and subtler realms to get lost in the noise. The third eye chakra can go to that "in-between" space to collect and get guidance and messages from the other world's spirits. In the presence of noise, you cannot hear the messages.

Therefore, you must cultivate silence of the mind and learn to handle overwhelming thoughts.

You can use various ways to calm and silence your mind, including meditation, indulging in your favorite hobby or art, or simply sitting calmly amid nature doing nothing but observing the surrounding beauty.

First, recognize how and when your intuition speaks to you. Usually, intuition is not loud and clear like a human voice. Instead, it sends subtle messages through slow-moving or flashes of imagery. Often, you will talk with your intuition, wondering how to get clarity about the received message. Sometimes, the messages come in goosebumps, an uncomfortable feeling in the gut, a sour taste in your mouth, or a sense of inexplicable relief. Often, the news could come as an emotion. For example, you intuitively like or hate someone you've just met. This could be your intuition, sending you a message about this person.

Just be alert to subtle forms of messages that your body and mind send you. To do that, you must connect with and talk with your inner voice. With practice, you will realize that you can easily catch on to the subtlest of hints that your intuition is trying to give you.

Try to Connect with Your Intuition Daily

Keep aside a dedicated time to connect with your intuition daily. Give time and effort to your intuitive powers and see what they are trying to tell you. This is especially important when you have to make a critical decision. However, to ensure you can understand your intuition's language, you must talk with it every day.

Write down what you felt or experienced when you tried connecting with your intuition. Don't leave it to your memory, at least in the initial stages of your learning experience. Write down what you felt, thought, and everything else when you sat down each day and connect with your intuition. The more practice you get, the better your skills will become.

Meditate as often as you can; the more profound your connection is with your intuition, the easier it will be to read and interpret its messages. Meditation is an excellent tool to deepen your relationship with your intuitive powers. Meditation teaches you to clear your mind and recognize the subtle impulses and signs your intuition is trying to give you.

And finally, learn to trust yourself and your intuitive powers. The more faith you have in your powers, the better outcomes you will get. Trust yourself because no one loves you more than you do. No one wants to see you happy and successful more than you do.

Build Your Creativity Skills

Each one of us is born with creativity. It is up to us to nurture, nourish and develop it to achieve our full potential. Creativity is a useful tool to eliminate rational fears and crutches that hold you down when you are, in reality, powerful to soar high in the clouds.

When your rational mind is relegated to the background, then the mental chatter also reduces, helping to achieve the calmness needed to communicate with your intuitive powers. When you can calm that part of your mind that wants to take charge of your life, you effectively open up numerous opportunities for yourself. Your third eye chakra has increased space to unfold, grow, and blossom.

Chapter 8. How to Increase Your Psychic Empath Abilities

Although you have psychic potential, you still have to train yourself so that your skills may become finely tuned. The following are some tips to help you enhance your psychic abilities:

Meditate Everyday

Meditation allows you to raise your vibration. The spirit energy vibrates at a high frequency. Through meditation, you can heighten your mental and spiritual powers and become capable of performing even greater psychic acts. Meditation is not a resource-intensive activity. You can pull it off almost anywhere. You just require a serene environment and some free time.

Communicate with Your Spirit Guide

Your spirit guide is basically an entity that protects you. They also enlighten you and make you insightful. When you call on their support, you will increase your chances of achieving what you desire. Have a sacred place in which you meet your spirit guide.

Use Psychometry

Psychometry is the practice of decoding the energies of an object. If you can become skilled in this discipline, you will receive a tremendous boost to your psychic abilities. Acquire an object that has sentimental value (e.g., a wedding band) and try to envision the energies of the owner.

Flower Visualization

To have strong psychic abilities, you have to improve your mind's eye. You can achieve this through flower visualization. The exercise entails picking up a few flowers and holding them in front of you. Now close your eyes and start envisioning each of them separately.

Random visualization

When you are done using the flower to strengthen your mind's eye, you may now explore some randomness. Just close your eyes, lie on your back in a serene environment and invite your spirit guides to show you many great wonders of the universe. Your spirit guides should show you magnificent images and videos.

Take a Walk in Nature

Psychics feel a tremendous connection with nature. You could take a stroll in a nature park while practicing mindful meditation. Take occasional stops by sweet-smelling flowers and savor their beauty. Lose yourself to the beauty of nature.

Eliminate Negativity

You cannot tap into your psychic powers if you harbor tons of negativity. Eliminate your negativity by heightening your self-awareness and being more forgiving to yourself. You also have to take the necessary steps to right the wrongs you have done. Once you're free of negativity, you're in the right headspace to employ your psychic powers.

Believe in Yourself

You cannot become a skilled clairvoyant unless you have tremendous belief in yourself. One of the ways of increasing your self-belief is through reading about those before you who have succeeded. Find books written by successful clairvoyants and read about them so that you can become familiar with their stories. Learn their tricks. The more you study about successful clairvoyants, the higher your odds of becoming successful yourself.

Rest

Quality rest is absolutely necessary. The more you rest, the more energy you have to channel into your psychic activities. One of the best ways to ensure quality rest is by getting enough sleep. You should get at least six hours of sleep every night. This will ensure that your mind is well rested and you're in top physical condition. Having enough rest is crucial for the development of your clairvoyant skills.

Try to Read Other People's Thoughts

This is a perfect way of strengthening your clairvoyant abilities. When you encounter someone, just gaze into their eyes and try to imagine what they are thinking about. If you can accurately read people's minds, then you can rest assured that your psychic abilities are very well developed.

Keep Track of Your Dreams

People with psychic abilities tend to dream a lot. After each dream, ensure you have noted it down in a journal. This will help you keep track of the dreams that came true. When you realize that your dreams are starting to become true, it indicates that your clairvoyant abilities are getting fine-tuned.

Improve Your Remote-Viewing Capability

Remote-viewing is the ability to view a place or an event through your mind's eye without you being physically present. To improve your ability of remote-viewing, you have to make good use of your imagination. Start with viewing places near you, and when you get them right, you can move on to far-flung places and objects.

Overcome Your Fears

If you have any fear in your mind, you will not achieve your full potential as a clairvoyant. You have to eliminate the fear to be able to channel all your mental energies in your psychic activities. The first step toward eliminating fear is to increase your knowledge. The more you know about a situation, the less ignorant you are and the more power and courage you acquire.

Resolve Your Differences with Those Around You

If you have problems with other people, ensure that you resolve them. You cannot achieve your full clairvoyant potential when you are not at peace with yourself or other people. Cast away the burden of bitterness and resolve your differences with those around you. This way, your mind is in a position to channel its energies into psychic activities.

Practice Seeing Auras

This is another great exercise for improving your psychic abilities. Have your friend stand next to a plain-colored wall. Then, look at them using your third eye. Notice if you get to see their auric field. If they have a high vibration, their aura will appear bright.

Ask a Friend to Call You

Contact your friend telepathically and ask them to give you a call. The more mental energy you invest in this activity, the more likely your friend will call you. If an empath developed their psychic potential, they could end up becoming so skilled that a career along that line would be in order.

Chapter 9. Psychic Protection

This is one of those topics that is pretty important but not something to really be afraid of. Here is where I tell you "yes, there are some scary and icky energies and entities out there," but they are nothing to be frightened of, especially if you take precautions and understand how to protect your energy.

We are going to skip the high-level metaphysical dialogue about how none of these energies are actually real and that you have just projected them through your mind because... People at our current vibrational level experience feel is genuine, so it is good to have some protection techniques against them.

One "secret" of the metaphysical world is that you are immensely stronger than you think you are. The goal is not to give away your power and instead realize that nothing can or will hurt or disturb you if you set firm boundaries. You are in control of your energy. Protect it, control it, and you will be fine.

All the methods I am going to talk about use the basic principle of energy and vibrations. Your mind has the power to change the vibratory frequency around you, just as different items in your household have different frequencies. Science is starting to catch up to this vibrational theory of reality that has been practiced for centuries by mystics and now is just labeling and categorizing common and widely used techniques.

Okay, now let's talk about some ways to protect your energy because there are a variety of different ways that individuals use it. The key is to pick what feels right for you and what works with your belief system and way of looking at the world. If something doesn't feel right, don't do it. If there is something else you prefer that I don't mention, go with that. At the essence and core of each of these methods, they remind you that you have power and control in any situation. And if you want, choose multiple ways (I do) and keep your energy nice and protected!

White Light

We are going to start with probably the most popular and very effective method that I highly recommend to anyone doing psychic work or really just going about your day. It may seem too simple to be true, but, in reality, this technique is highly productive, and there is a reason that almost every single book on psychic work will teach this method.

To put white light around you, all you do is see the image of a white light surrounding your body in your mind's eye. It sounds a little too simple, right?!! Well, we can add a little to this to help you reinforce the idea and make your bubble stronger and more protective. Here is a little exercise you can do:

1. First, close your eyes and take a few breaths to center yourself and go into your body. Feel yourself calming down. Feel the energy flowing down your spine, down your feet,

and out into the ground. See how far down you can push that energy.

2. Now, feel yourself bringing energy from your feet up through your legs, up to your spine, and into your heart. Keep that energy there.

3. Next, feel your energy coming into the top of your head, down your neck, and into your heart. Pull the energy in with your breath.

4. Now, see those two energies as a ball of white light in your heart. Take your breath and push that energy out around your body. Feel and see in your mind's eye the energy as white light surrounding your body.

5. Some individuals may feel warmer at this point as the energy engulfs their bodies. You may feel a tingling sensation or nothing at all. In your mind, see this white light as a bubble of protection shielding you from outside energies.

Once you practice this method a few times, you will find that it is very easy and can be a quick method. Whenever you feel "off" or "scared" or need some protection, this is a great technique to do. When I used to work in an office with other people, I would do this in my car before getting out to prepare myself for the energies I might encounter. For empaths, this is also helpful to implement before going into any location with a lot of energy, aka people.

Prayer or Mantra

Another very effective method to help protect your energy is to say a prayer or a mantra. This method also works well with the white light method, and many times people combine the two. Setting your intention for protection and raising to a place of love will help you keep your energy free of any negativity.

Any prayer that you feel called to will work, as long as you believe it and it works with your mindset. The Lord's Prayer or a few Hail Mary's are wonderful tools. Both have high vibrations and help raise the energy of the individual saying them. Mantras are also great tools, and if you have one you are drawn to, I would recommend using that. Personally, I use the mantra "May all beings be happy" or "Sabbe Satta Suhki Hontu" to center my energy and bring myself to a higher level that offers protection. Additionally, you may find it helpful to come up with your own mantra or prayer to say before you engage in any psychic work. It sets your intentions for the job you are going to do and that you would like to be protected during that work.

These methods work well for protection, and you can use them in combination with each other or separately. Again, this is all about what works best for you.

Sacred Smoke

Sacred smoke is another one of those methods that have been used for years and in various cultures to offer protection to individuals. Perhaps the most widely used smoke for protection and cleansing nowadays is that of a smudge stick or sage. It has become so accustomed and a symbol of the New Age community that sometimes I think people forget that it is actually a powerful tool.

Sage bundled together in a smudge stick or loose-leaf sage works fantastic to cleanse the air in the space you are located. If you feel heavy or negative energy is in an environment, this tool effectively clears that energy out. I find that using it as a preventative measure to prepare the place you are using for readings is also helpful as it discourages negative energy from settling in that environment.

This is not the only method of smoke that works to purify the energy or the environment. I have also found frankincense and myrrh to be great tools to protect working spaces. You may even recognize different traditional religious organizations use this as well. You can also pick an incense that you feel drawn to or even change it up for different types of work you do. When I first started this work, I tried various fragrances to see which vibration I preferred and what worked best for my work. I even use different scents for different tasks depending on what I want to accomplish.

Crystals

Crystals have seemed to become ubiquitous in the metaphysical and New Age community, and there is a good reason for that. Crystals emit vibrations that help to change the nature and field of the environment you are in. Some crystals are also well known to help protect the energy or field of individuals. You will usually find crystals that offer more protective qualities are dark-colored in nature, typically black. There is a variety out there, and this is another case in which you want to try out some or hold different specimens and see what feels right for you. In the end, it doesn't matter what any book says or even what I write here; what works for you and what you feel drawn to will always be best.

In general, some popular crystals to use for protection include black tourmaline, smokey quartz, obsidian, and jasper. You can place crystals in the environment in which you do your psychic work; some individuals like to wear crystals in jewelry or carry them as pocket stones. Again, broken record here, do what feels right for yourself.

Another tip I have for finding crystals is to look to see if there are a gem and mineral shows around you. If you are in a big city, there is a chance that there may be one of these shows that happen once or twice a year. You will usually find more variety and lower prices at these shows than in traditional metaphysical stores. I have watched over the past decade as the prices of these stones have increased as interest has, and price gouging is something to watch out for.

Candles

Candles are another tremendous protective tool that has been used throughout the years, and they are also pretty easy to come by. Candles provide fire and the symbol of light. Like the white light method above, the use of symbolic candles shows a predisposition towards the "light" instead of the "dark."

You can use different colored candles for different types of readings or practices, and you can also choose between unscented candles and those that provide a fragrance. Some individuals even sell candles that contain crystals, herbs, and prayer intentions already in them. Finding pre-made candles with protective energies already imbued is a great idea, or, even better, you can create them yourself.

Don't discount the plain white unscented candle, though. Although it may look simple and boring, a standard candle with no additions can be a potent tool. You may find that lighting a candle before you begin any work sets the intention for protection in your space and helps you get into the correct mindset.

Talismans

The idea of protective talismans has been around for centuries, but currently, they are not very popular. A protective talisman is simply an item that has been imbued with the energy and intention to provide protection. These can come in many different forms ranging from necklaces to items passed down from earlier generations. You may feel a connection to an old trinket that your grandfather carried around or something he kept in his wallet. Using this as a talisman and asking that grandfather to provide protection can assist your energetic field.

Chapter 10. How to Stop Negative Energy and Stress

If you've at any point invested some energy with an antagonistic individual, you know how rapidly you can begin to take on that negative mindset. Have you at any point felt that you wish you had realized how to shield yourself from negative energy?

Now and then, it happens that individuals don't understand they have gotten adverse because of being around antagonistic individuals. Also, pessimistic individuals are the most exceedingly awful. If you are feeling overpowered from assuming the negative energy of others, there is an approach to prevent it from occurring. Here are the means by which to shield yourself from engrossing others' negative energy so you can continue ahead with living a more positive and gainful life.

Identify Whose Emotion Is Present

When a negative feeling assumes control, it's critical to identify the source. Is it your own negative feeling or did you get it from another person? If it is yours, then you can manage it and work through those feelings; however, if it is somebody else's, you have to perceive that it's not your weight to convey and release it.

Put Some Distance Between You and the Negativity

Head outside, go for a stroll, have lunch in your vehicle, whatever you need to do to part with yourself some space from the antagonism and the adverse individuals, do it. Now and again, all you need is a couple of moments to refocus your considerations and advise yourself that their cynicism isn't your antagonism.

Know Your Limits

When it comes to managing pessimism and negative energy, it's critical to comprehend what triggers that feeling in you. When you can identify an inclination related to antagonism, you can identify it sooner and manage it quicker. If that antagonism is related to an individual, you can see it originating from a mile away and begin strolling the other way.

Just Breathe

If you have an inclination that you are getting overpowered by negative feelings, energy, or another person's adverse feeling or energy, then take a couple of moments to direct your breathing and reset your considerations.

Meditate

If negative feelings and energy are streaming over you, take a couple of moments to sit discreetly in your own head and reflect. Square the negative considerations and prepare for the positive feelings and energy in your life.

Get Clear with People

When it comes to overseeing antagonistic energy and pessimistic individuals, once in a while you simply need to lay down the law and state "no." The word no has a great deal of intensity that we often underestimate. It can leave somebody speechless when it is utilized effectively. If somebody is attempting to take your daylight, defining cutoff points and limits with that individual can go far to changing the tune of their tune when they are around you. You are permitted to instruct them to stop.

Chapter 11. Dream Interpretation

Empaths often are lucid dreamers. Interpreting dreams can help you to find their relevance in physical life. This can be proof of how strong your spiritual side is. This means that there is an ability to shift through dimensions and connect with energies that are beyond the limits of normal understanding.

Free-fall dreams are also common for empaths. These types of dreams connect with releasing spiritual energies. They also are up to interpretation because many believe that it means strength to stand up for themselves in waking life must be found. Sequential dreams can be very structured and events in the dreams can be connected. These chronicle events are used to bring an understanding of a potential real-life event.

Creative dreams can come across as sources of inspiration. Empaths can get ideas from their dream worlds and bring them into their lives. Having a vivid imagination and lots of experience with multiple forms of energy, empaths can experience very creative and vivid dream worlds. Nightmares can be very disturbing and haunting to them. Because they are sensitive beings, even the smallest details can settle into a permanent place in their minds until they resolve them. Performing sleep meditations and energy-clearing techniques before resting can help to bring forth positive dreams.

Having the ability to process and deal with the emotional stress that intense dreams can bring forth is important for empaths. Most of them will be able to define dreams with clarity and understand when their dreams are mirroring their subconscious and spiritual realities. Before realizing that one is an empath, it's quite easy for them to go through life as an unsuspecting energy sponge. Those that are unaware of their abilities will take on these emotions and energies everywhere they go without understanding why. This can lead to suddenly feeling sick or becoming overwhelmed with anxiety or sadness even when there is nothing around to cause this feeling. You must develop specific self-care skills and protection techniques to manage your empathic nature and prevent overload. Bringing awareness into your body becomes extremely important. Find activities and exercises that bring you back into your body and the present moment. As an empath, you may experience nervous system overdrive, and it's important that you notice the signs and take the steps to remedy them. Breathing techniques that bring the heart rate down and return to your baseline. Be careful to take stock of how you feel after you spend time with others. It won't take long to learn what people and situations are hazardous to your well-being.

One method of self-care for living as an empath is to get in touch with and unblock your chakras. If you are familiar with the 7 chakras, you understand how you can manage the energy and emotions in your body through them. In just a few minutes a day, you can clear all stored energy and strengthen all these energetic centers. An easy way to do this is to concentrate on a chakra while meditating and perform breathing exercises, visualizing that you are pulling clear, clean energy into the area and breathing out all negative, and stored energies from the area. Many stretches focus on balancing and aligning chakras, and yoga can be extremely helpful for empaths who are feeling overwhelmed. Unblock energies and keep them flowing freely.

Common Dreams and Their Interpretation

Dreams About Falling

Most of us have dreamt about falling from great heights at least once in our lives. It is a very common and scary dream and some people believe that you should not hit the ground in this dream because you will die. Of course, this is just a myth and there is no truth in it! So, what does it mean?

Dream experts have linked this dream with problems in the dreamer's life. They say that it is a sign that something is getting out of control. It means that you need to amend the choices you have made or take a different direction in some parts of your life. It could also signify fear and anxiety that you have over a certain situation in your life like in your place of work or your relationship.

Dream About Being Late

Have you ever dreamt of being late and missing some opportunities? This dream can be very stressful and frustrating. This symbolizes the anxieties that you have in your life. You could be scared about upcoming changes or you are worried if you can finish the projects that you are working on. If you dream of being late for appointments or dates, then it means that you are overwhelmed by work so much that you do not have enough time for yourself. If it is about getting late for the airport and missing a flight, then it means your time is not enough for you to finish what you are doing. Therefore, the best remedy for this is just to take enough work that you can handle.

Dreams About Wanting to Use the Bathroom but You Can't Find the Toilet

Dreaming about looking for a toilet when we want to use it can be frustrating. In this dream, you may find that when you try to relieve yourself somewhere you find that some people are looking at you. The feeling here can be shameful yet the call of nature is pushing you to find a place. Dream experts suggest that this could be a representation of the anxieties and fear that we are having in our lives. It could also be a sign that we are not allowing ourselves the basic needs in our lives. It means that we are too busy attending to the needs of other people that we forget our own. It could also mean that we have a problem expressing ourselves in our waking life.

Dreaming About Snakes

Dreaming of seeing snakes or being bitten by them can be very frightening. Most of us have had this dream at some point in our lives, so what does it mean? This dream has a different interpretation for different people and different situations. This could signify some worries or fears in your waking life that require attention. However, most dream experts suggest that this dream symbolizes temptations, danger, and forbidden sexuality. Snakes symbolize healing and transformation and it can be a sign of warning that something bad will happen. Being chased by snakes means that you are running from something that needs your attention.

If the snake chasing you is a wild one, then it signifies that something in your life is getting out of control; this could be your health or relationship. If the dream is about fighting with a snake, then it means that you are opposing some changes or situations in your life. This could be something that you do not want to happen or something that happened, but you do not like. If you dream of a snake biting you, then it means you are facing hard times, which can destroy you so you need to take action immediately.

Dreams About Taking an Exam

This is a very common dream for those who are out of school and those who work performance-related jobs. It is associated with self-criticism and the desire to achieve higher expectations in life. Dream interpreters claim that this dream signifies anxiety and fear of failure. It can also symbolize an upcoming event that requires you to make decisions or a new phase in your life. It could also mean that you are suffering from low self-esteem or low self-confidence and you fear that you are not handling life challenges the way you should.

Dreams About Being Pregnant

This is another dream that has multiple interpretations. It symbolizes new beginnings and new challenges. Loewenberg, a dream expert, believes that this is a positive dream and it symbolizes some growth and development in a woman's potential. It also represents the birth of a new idea, direction, or project. It could also represent a woman's fear of becoming an inadequate mother in her parenting. This dream is associated with an increase in finances, the flowering of romance, great change.

Dreams About Flying

Dreams about flying can be fascinating as well as scary if you fear great heights. This dream has had different interpretations. Some dream experts suggest that it represents freedom and independence and it could mean that you are trying to escape from some situations in your life. Other dream experts claim that if you are unable to fly in this dream, it means that you are straining to achieve your set goals, or something is preventing you from reaching your target in life. They suggest that flying alone represents independence and freedom from social restraints or you have released yourself from those things that have been weighing you down.

Dreams About a Cheating Partner

This dream can be very worrying, and it can make someone ask themselves the question "what if it's true?" So what's the deeper meaning of this distressing dream for couples?

Dream experts suggest that having such dreams does not mean that your partner is cheating or will cheat. It could be reflections of the fear you have for infidelity or maybe you have been cheated on before and you fear that it might happen again. You could be testing the limits of reality! Such dreams also symbolize that there are trust issues in your relationship and there is a gap in communication. Not spending enough time with your partner because of job commitments or distance can also lead to such dreams. It could also be a sign that something needs correction in your relationship.

Dreams About Losing Teeth

This dream has different interpretations. Some dream experts believe that teeth symbolize power and confidence, so the dream could mean that the dreamer has lost confidence and the ability to be assertive and decisive, maybe because of what happened in their lives. To some, it is a sign of a broken relationship, a fulfillment of becoming pregnant, and it could mean sexual stimulation for men. Some interpreters also suggest that this dream could signify doubt about one's attractiveness and appearance. It could also represent anxiety about communicating something or fear that one might have said something embarrassing.

Dreams About Being Naked in Public

It can be frustrating to dream that you are showing up in your workplace or school naked! Dream experts suggest that this kind of dream represents feelings of vulnerability, insecurity, shame, and humiliation. This is common for individuals who have landed a new job that involves coming into public view.

Dreams About Dying

This is a horrifying dream, and most people will wake up from the dream crying. You can dream about the death of your relative or a friend. Some people believe that if you keep such dreams to yourself, it would happen! However, this is not true. Dream interpreters suggest that this dream signifies anxiety about change. It can happen if you are scared of changes because you do not know what will happen on the other side of change. Therefore, it is simply the mourning of the inevitable passage of time. This dream could also mean that the dreamer wishes to end something bothering them in their life. This could be a stressful job, relationship, or a past that is haunting them. Some experts believe that this is not a dream but an encouragement to pursue new endeavors.

Dreams About Being Chased

Have you ever dreamt of being chased by an unknown attacker, but you feel your legs are heavy and slowing you down? This is a very common and terrifying dream. What is its deeper meaning? Dream experts claim that this dream means that you have some things you are trying to run from in your life. It could be a desire to escape from your fears!

If you dream that you are being attacked but you cannot run no matter how much you try, then it signifies that you are suffering from low self-esteem and low self-confidence. It could also mean that you are in a situation where you are powerless.

The interpretation of this dream will depend on the identity of the attacker. If it is an animal, then it could mean you are running from your own emotions and passions. If it is an unknown attacker, then it signifies your fears of your childhood abuses and trauma, and if the attacker is someone from the opposite sex, then you are afraid of love. This could be a result of an abusive past relationship.

Chapter 12. Mediumship

In this chapter, we will talk about medium reading. So, what's the difference? Well, someone who does psychic readings may not have mediumistic abilities, which are acting as a vessel and a bridge of communication between the spirit world and the world of the living, but all mediums have psychic abilities, as this is what they use to contact the spirits of the dead.

Mediumship or mediums may be a term you haven't heard before. A medium is a person who is a bridge between the dead and the living. They can communicate with those that have passed over and convey messages to the living for them. If you've ever used an Ouija board, this is one form of mediumship, as you are contacting, or attempting to contact, the spirits of the dead—although Ouija boards are usually used as a form of entertainment more than anything serious.

The forms of mediumship used by practicing mediums are when the spirit of the dead speaks through the medium, and when the medium receives messages clairvoyantly (or clairsentiently, claircognizantly, clairaudiently), relays the message to the living. Most often the medium is asked by a living person to try and contact and create a channel of communication with a dead loved one because they miss them and/or because there are unfinished business or unanswered questions between them and they want a sense of closure. The spirit of the dead loved one likely feels the same so these sessions can be very healing.

If you wish to become a medium, an intermediary between the spirit world and the living, you will need to have a stronghold on the four intuitive types (even if you favor one more than the others) as the messages will come through, and you will perceive them via clairvoyance, clairaudience, clairsentience or claircognizance. This is something to try once you've been practicing your psychic abilities for a while and feel confident. You can still be on a beginner's path, but make sure you've got the basics down. If you feel that you are a natural psychic medium, someone who has sensed the presence of spirits of the dead from a young age, then you may already have an idea of how to communicate and use these spirit channels. This is not a necessity to becoming a medium, however.

If you know any mediums, or if you find that there is a local practicing medium you can get in touch with, ask them about their craft. How does it feel to communicate with spirits? When did they start or when did they first notice they had this ability? What are some examples of mediumistic experiences they've had? You can also search online to read first-hand experiences from mediums if there are none you can contact where you live. Just be careful that the person you are learning from is not a scam artist, as the world of psychic practice is rife with frauds looking to exploit people for money.

To begin practice towards contacting spirits, you must be in a state of total relaxation. Find a calm, comfortable spot, without bright lights. Feel the energy of the universe flowing through you and relax your mind, letting other thoughts that poke at you fade away. Now it's time to call upon the spirits. Before you do this next step, make sure you've mastered psychic protection against negative spirits and entities as it's possible to accidentally invite a negative spirit into your home. To help reduce the risk of a negative spirit entering your space, think of a specific deceased loved one of yours that you would like to contact (this can also be a pet). That way, your call is not extended to any spirit who happens to be around. They are not invited, only your loved one's spirit is. Now call upon them out loud. Ask them into your space and maybe ask a question of them or ask if they have anything to communicate. Call upon them mentally too. Summon up an image of them in your mind, quite detailed, and mentally welcome them into space. If you feel their presence, ask them a question you have prepared beforehand. You may sense them in different ways, whether you smell the cologne they used to wear, hear their laugh or a song they used to sing, see their favorite color or a piece of clothing they used to wear in your mind's eye, or a sudden shift of emotion where you feel warm and full of love. These are just examples to show you that the way you sense them may not be seeing their image speaking to you in your mind's eye. The way they answer the questions may be through images that must be interpreted or through words you see or hear in your mind. If you answer a question and get a strong emotion immediately afterward, this may also be a response. Or if they answer claircognizantly, then you will just know the answer. Remember not to force or make up their presence or answers. Just let them flow, and if they don't show up or answer any questions, then that's okay. Just keep reaching out and practicing and stay relaxed. If you pick up nothing, don't force it. Release and try again another time.

You can also try practicing as a medium for a friend, and you can call upon the spirit of their loved one, asking the spirit any questions your friend may have of them. If you really want to challenge yourself, don't ask your friend who is the person they want to contact. Go in blind. Ask them only to picture and think about the person they wish to contact. Keep your mind clear and relaxed, and be open and receptive to any energies and messages you may receive. If images or feelings start popping up, describe them to your friend. You can go online and look up videos of psychics in action to see how this is done. For example, if you're sitting there with an empty mind and all of a sudden a figure of a man pops into your mind, and then the color red, and then the concept of Thanksgiving dinner, and the smell of cigarettes, you would say, "I'm seeing a man, now the color red, and something to do with Thanksgiving. I also smell cigarettes." You obviously will not know what this means, so ask your friend if it has any significance for them. After all, when acting as a medium, the message isn't for you but for the other person the spirit of the dead is connected to. If this is a legitimate message your friend will get it right away, and if they feel like it, they can tell you what it means to them. Maybe the man was their uncle whose favorite color or shirt or car was red, and he always hosted a big family Thanksgiving at his house, it was an annual family tradition. And he smoked, which was a familiar and comforting reminder of his presence to all who knew him. This is an example of how a medium reading may progress. You may hear words or phrases from the deceased as well that you should relay to the living person. Tell them everything you see and hear in your message, even if it may not make sense to you, as it may make sense and be important to them. If not, then just keep going. You probably won't get everything right, especially since you are just beginning, so just keep telling them what you are sensing and make sure you aren't forcing these messages. Make sure they are coming to you naturally and clearly from the spirit you have contacted.

Chapter 13. Guided Meditation Sessions

Guided Meditation Session for Repelling Energy Vampires

Ever feel drained, fatigued, and have a hard time going to sleep? There is a good chance that the energy vampires in your life may be keeping you up at night. If this sounds like you, consider giving meditation a try! There are many different ways of meditating; some focus on the breath to encourage more oxygen flow into your system while others channel all of their mental and physical energy inward in order to heal themselves. By meditating regularly, it's possible that you can become less susceptible to these negative forces!

Take a moment today for yourself by trying this guided meditation session from life hack. Set aside about 20 minutes so that you can release any pent-up anger or stress.

1. Sit in a comfortable position.
2. Close your eyes and take a deep breath. Exhale as you count to 5. Inhale as you count to 10, and repeat this cycle several times.
3. Focus on the tips of your fingers and feel the energy build-up within. Then, let it all out by intentionally creating sparks between your fingertips. Take another deep breath before

continuing with this process until you've reached a state of pure relaxation.

4. Pray for safety while clearing negative energies from your home and workplace. Think of it as a sort of house/life energy cleansing.

5. Ask for help from above by calling on your deity of choice. Ask that the near future will be free from evil and that you will be able to protect yourself and others around you from any further negative vibes. Continue with the mantra, "I am safe" until you feel completely calm.

6. Breathe in deeply for 5 seconds, and then breathe out for 7 seconds while imagining a white light entering your body through your crown chakra (the top of your head). Try to focus your mind on the light and try to create energy with your hands. Repeat until you feel at one with the universe.

7. While surrounded by the pure white light, ask for a positive energy source to come into your life, whether it is a new friend, lover, or mentor.

8. Say goodbye to any negative spirits by visualizing them leaving your body through the top of your head and dissolving into thin air.

9. Breathe in deeply for 5 seconds and then breathe out for 7 seconds while imagining a white light being absorbed back into your body through the crown chakra on top of your head. Continue this visualization until you feel recharged.

10. Take another deep breath and repeat this entire process one more time.

11. End by visualizing a bright, white light at the base of your spine, and then say goodbye to any other negative spirits. Once you've released all of the negative energy in your body, you will feel refreshed and at peace with yourself and the universe.

12. Light a candle before beginning this meditation session to cleanse your home or workplace of any additional negative energy that may remain after you've finished moving out. If there has been any sign of poltergeist activity in your location, be sure to remove all traces of candles, statues, incense sticks, or anything else that might have been touched by an evil spirit from the premises.

After you're finished, record your experience and share it with a friend. This meditation session can be repeated every single day in order to build up your defense against any negative entities.

Guided Meditation Session for Emotion Realignment

1. Find a quiet space where you can sit comfortably. Close your eyes and take three deep breaths, in and out.

2. Once you feel relaxed, begin to think of a person who helps bring balance to your life. It could be a teacher or mentor. It could be a friend or family member that you know is always there for you when times get tough.

3. Imagine that person in your mind's eye. Really feel their presence and the positive energy they bring when they are around you.

4. Picture yourself as this person in your mind's eye, embodied with their compassion, strength, and positivity.
5. Breathe in their energy as you hold the image of them in your mind. Feel your mind and body relax as you do this.
6. Breathe out any negativity or anxiety that is present in your mind or body.
7. Feel the tension and stress leave you as you focus on this image.
8. Imagine yourself in a safe place, free from all stresses or dangers. You can be anywhere here, but feel most comfortable.
9. Feel the tension leave you and your body relaxed more as you hold the image of this person. You feel more relaxed as you continue to relax and breathe.
10. Keep breathing in their energy until you feel fully relaxed.
11. Imagine that this person is with you now, helping bring balance and peace into your daily life. Feel them here helping to calm and ground your mind, body, or emotions.
12. Keep breathing in their energy until you feel completely relaxed.
13. Picture yourself in a safe place, free from all stresses or dangers. You can be anywhere here, but feel most comfortable. Feel the tension leave you and your body relaxed more as you hold the image of this person. You feel more relaxed as you continue to relax and breathe.
14. Focus on this image of yourself for a few minutes before opening your eyes. Have a Zen moment by discarding

negative thoughts from your mind or body, then get up and carry on with your day!

Guided Meditation for Clearing Your Energy/Aura

1. Sit comfortably in a quiet place. Take a few deep breaths and bring your attention to your breath as it enters and leaves your body.
2. Think of a question you have about yourself or the world around you. Bring this question into your mind and form an intention to have it answered during this meditation experience.
3. Bring your awareness to your lower belly, roughly three inches below the navel. You can visualize this area at the center of your body below the navel, or you might want to place one hand over this area if it feels more comfortable for you.
4. Bring your awareness to this area as you breathe in.
5. When your breath is fully inhaled, visualize the breath passing through this area and the energy that surrounds it. As you breathe out, imagine a wave of energy flowing from this center outward. It flows farther than you look. It passes through everything you have ever touched or experienced and enters other people and places. Whatever it touches, from an atom in the core of a planet to a single cell in the body of a person, is affected by your aura. Its energy

surrounds them and affects their life journey as well as their experience of living on Earth at any given moment.

6. Visualize your aura spreading out and touching everything in its path.

7. Take a few moments to visualize your aura touching everything around you, surrounding you with positive energy. Allow the vibrations of the universe to flow into the energy that surrounds you as you breathe in and out.

8. As your focus turns to your breath, bring awareness to that same area of your lower belly where you were visualizing the aura entering and leaving your body.

9. Feel this area fill with energy again as you inhale and exhale, but this time imagine it filling up with light, heat, or love—whatever it is that most make sense for you at this moment. Give it a color if it makes sense for you to do so.

10. Visualize this area filled with a warm glowing light—the light of love and compassion. This is the light of love that exists at the center of your being. Allow it to expand to fill your entire body.

11. As you breathe in, visualize energy gathering from the center outward. Feel this energy filling you up like a balloon or an inflated tire until you are completely full of light, heat, and love.

12. As you breathe out, visualize this warmth coming out through your hands, fingers, and toes and moving into the room around you as well as spreading through the objects and people in it. As it moves into everything it touches, they

are all filled with warmth and light and begin emanating their own energy as well.

13. For a few minutes or so, continue to breathe in and out while focusing on this area of your body, filling and emptying yourself with light, heat, and love.

14. When you are ready to finish your meditation practice, bring your awareness back to the area below your navel. Take a deep breath in and feel the energy flowing in from the center of the universe. As you breathe out slowly through pursed lips, imagine all the light, heat, or love that you have filled yourself with during this meditation flowing back into this core area of your being. It is stored there for safekeeping as part of who you are at any given moment.

15. Take another deep breath in and fill yourself with love.

16. When you are ready, slowly open your eyes. Deeply enjoy the feeling of love and compassion that is inside you right now. If this is the first time you have meditated using these guided imagery techniques or if this is your first guided meditation, you may want to imagine yourself at a beautiful outdoor location filled with trees, grass, flowers—you get the idea. In whichever case, take some time to enjoy this feeling as you open your eyes and return to the world around you.

Enjoy this feeling of warmth and love in your life today. Then, continue to use it to transform your life and the lives around you, allowing it to spread from you into everything that you touch.

Guided Meditation to Create an Energy Shield

Everybody has some sort of an energy shield. It can be a simple bubble or a complicated force field. The reason behind it is to protect you from the outside world and from your own emotions. Guided meditation for creating an energy shield is about visualizing the shape and color of this protective barrier to help you create one for real in your life. Meditation helps calm down your body, mind, and emotions so that you can get into a state where it's easier to do things like visualize things or change something as complex as an energy shield. You will need:

1. A quiet place where you won't be distracted or disturbed and time to yourself.
2. To be in a comfortable position (you should feel at ease, neither too relaxed nor too tense).
3. To be in a well-lit room or to have the light on inside you (some people prefer to add some sort of ambient lighting—candle, incense, low light).
4. If you want to use guided meditation for creating an energy shield to guard your home or other places, you'll need to do the same routine every day.

You can also use it as a meditation for moving energy around yourself or clearing a room.

1. Clear your mind, and through that space where there is nothing, sit comfortably in a lotus posture that allows you to feel relaxed but be awake at the same time.

2. Close your eyes after setting out on a deep breath, and begin breathing deeply while keeping your eyes closed after inhaling.

   NOTE: Part of this activity is about visualizing certain things—so you will need both visualization and breathing at the same time.

3. Now imagine an energy shield around you. Visualize the SHAPE and COLOR of this shield and how it surrounds your body.

4. For those who want to experience this guided meditation on creating an energy shield, visualize two (or three) glass balls forming a pyramid shape, and on top of it, you'll see the color you want your shield to be: for example, blue, pink, green, silver, etc.

5. For those who want to use this guided meditation for moving energy around themselves, they can imagine that they are standing under a strong colored light with their backs turned towards it so that they don't get burned by its intensity or feel suffocated by its presence (that would be like looking at the sun). They will then imagine the energy from that light touching them on the back and moving around their bodies. And for those who want to use this guided meditation for clearing a room, will imagine that they are standing in the middle of a green forest (or open space—wherever they feel most relaxed). Light is coming from the sky, touching their bodies and healing them from all negativity they have ever experienced. After clearing

one's self, this light moves towards the places where you want to clear the room from negative energy.

6. They are now standing under that powerful sphere of healing light, taking a few deep breaths while feeling its warmth or silvery/golden glow embracing them in every breath.

7. When you're done, open your eyes, take a few deep breaths and stretch yourself.

If you are in the middle of any stressful activity (job, school, opening a business, or facing any other challenge), you can use this guided meditation for creating an energy shield to minimize the effects (turning it into something small) that will distract you from what's really important—moving on toward your ambitious goals. And if you need to create an energy shield for your home or even neighborhood, it's best to create one every day when you wake up in the morning and before going to bed at night around where people live (not necessarily everyone but some of them).

Chapter 14. Astral Projection and Remote Viewing

Astral Projection

We have the potential to project ourselves out of our physical bodies while sleeping, a process known as astral projection. Despite the fact that they appear to be far-fetched and perhaps even a little realistic, the literature has documented some successful occurrences of real-world astral projection. As you sleep or meditate intensely, your soul (or astral body) disappears and returns to your physical body. After your spirit has been ejected from your body, you are free to roam wherever you desire.

According to Healthline, unlike astral projections, out-of-body experiences (OBEs) are frequently unplanned. To begin, when someone has an out-of-body experience, their spirit or consciousness floats above and around their body. In contrast, with projections, the consciousness is actively guided to a different area. Second, while astral projection is largely a spiritual practice, out-of-body experiences have been primarily recognized in the medical field.

The subject of whether or not astral projection is a safe technique is frequently raised. When it comes to astral projection, the answer is the same as it is for any other dangerous sport: if done with caution, preparation, and information beforehand, it is absolutely safe. In some situations, astral projections, on the other hand, may be harmful. In contrast, astral projection can be completely safe and even useful! Consider whether you'd like to learn something new that you haven't done before. Because astral projections affect both your physical body and your soul, you may suffer from severe psychological and physical consequences in this situation.

Consider astral projection to be a sport or something similar in terms of accessibility. Almost everyone can prepare to project astrologically with proper knowledge and caution. Furthermore, when it comes to astral projection, some persons will naturally require less time and effort to achieve the same results as others. The following recommendation may be useful: have a lot of patience. While it's reasonable to desire to practice astral projection in real life from time to time, you should always follow your instincts and wait until you've mastered all of the delicate details of astral projection. For people who don't have the patience to be guided repeatedly during the learning process, astral projection may not be the best option right now.

Mastering the technique of astral projection will take a long time. It will take time to learn, practice, and experiment with different methods; you will not do everything right the first time. If you don't give up after one or two false attempts, you'll almost likely learn how to project correctly in the end. To maximize the benefit of your desired study, you must guarantee that you have the time to commit to it.

According to studies, people aged 13 to 18 have a natural advantage in the realm of astral projection. This is not to say that older individuals can't learn to project; rather, it implies that young people are more receptive, making it easier for them to suspend disbelief and learn about astral projections.

Even if you are well-versed in the specifics of what astral projection is and how to perform it, your preliminary efforts may not be successful, no matter how much and how hard you try. That is why you should experiment with various tactics, strategies, and approaches. If your first attempts at achievement fail, keep trying. This attempt was not overlooked. They just serve to prepare you for the next level when you will be able to command your spirit beyond the boundaries of your physical body. You can only learn how to perform anything correctly if you practice it. There are no other options for learning. There are various erroneous methods for avoiding astral projections, and practice and experimentation are your best friends.

It's a good idea to experiment with projection first if you suspect something will be tough before you begin studying it. Despite the fact that they are all true, a number of incidents have been treated with skepticism.

The scenario is essentially similar when it comes to astral projections. If you went into the experiment with preconceived assumptions about why astral projections are false and then sought to justify your intuition, you would fail terribly. You're making an attempt to refute a claim made by tens of thousands of other people. If you approach this with an open mind and allow yourself to investigate and experiment with new ideas, you will greatly increase your chances of success.

The Methodology of Astral Screening

Not only must you prepare yourself and your thoughts for astral projections, but you must also create a receptive environment. Here are a few basic techniques to make a projection-friendly environment:

Choose a Location

To begin, think about the fundamentals: where do you anticipate often locating your projects? In terms of transportation, how accessible is it?

Your bed: You may discover that projecting from your bed is the most convenient alternative. This atmosphere will not tense your muscles, and it is one in which you are already comfortable and secure in your ability to operate. Furthermore, many individuals prefer to finish watching movies right before going to bed, which is why beds are a perfect option than sofas. Furthermore, unlike in other more limited situations where you can project, if you are lying in bed, you are not concerned about your body falling out. However, there are certain disadvantages to sleeping on your bed that should be considered in addition to the benefits. In this case, you may be able to put your body to sleep before it separates from your soul if you do it from your bed, as this is the location your body is naturally associated with sleeping. Furthermore, if you share a bed with another person, it may not be the best place to sleep because the other person may interfere with your projection efforts on purpose or inadvertently.

If you choose this place, your living room sofa is going to be an outstanding choice for your specified space, mostly since you will be able to layout it for your convenience. This means that your body may develop a psychological attachment to the area to the point where it feels as though it is sitting on its sofa whenever it is time to project. This will be impossible if you project from your bed. Furthermore, because you would be alone in this environment, there would be very few distractions for you to cope with. If your sofa has rough, uncomfortable cushions or a back alignment that irritates you, it may not be the best location to sit and relax. Try altering the cushions, adding a blanket, and moving the furniture before starting the project to make the surroundings as comfortable as possible.

If you don't want to project while lying down, you might find that projecting from your chair is a better option than sitting up. It's a terrific option because you won't fall asleep if you project from your chair during the entire. Furthermore, you will almost surely be alone in your chair, which means no irritating traffic or people interfering with your duties.

However, in addition to its benefits, the projection of a straight chair has a number of significant disadvantages. Your body is more likely to fall into this position, causing it to be pushed out of the projection state and depositing your astral self back into your physical body before you have a chance. Otherwise, your head may flop up over your neck, depriving you of a consistent source of oxygen and potentially leading to severe breathing problems if the scenario persists for an extended amount of time.

Regardless of the mix of these three you choose, the idea is to establish a posture in which you feel safe and where your astral self may effortlessly enter and exit your body without generating any external interference or hindrance (or even a choice).

Start Keeping a Journal of Your Activities

When you first begin experimenting with astral projection, it's a good idea to keep a journal of your experiences. You'll have to be quite cautious if you want to keep this going. If you have an astral experience, write down all you remember so that you can later use it to figure out patterns and improve your project skills.

1. Begin by noting the impending event's date and time. When did it take place? What did you do immediately before or after you projected? You've most likely tried it out on a weekend or a vacation. Keeping track of all of this will allow you to discover the optimum time and day to generate your most effective forecasts, allowing you to select the most appropriate dates for your future forecast.
2. Before you begin, make a list of the events and conditions that transpired before your forecast. What occurred in the seconds preceding your attempt? Have you ever gotten out of bed after a particularly boozy night? If your screening was beneficial, you can try to recreate these events in the

future and try to replicate the experience while planning your next move.

3. Take detailed notes on anything that occurs throughout the screening. Keep a mental record of what transpired. Did you notice any temperature variations throughout your visit, for example? Do you get a tingling sensation throughout your body? Have you ever heard a high-pitched sound or an external voice, along with the sensation of being joined in your ascension? When you projected your thoughts, you most certainly saw other beings. All of this helps you keep control of your experiences and ensures that your projections and expectations are not influenced by detrimental external forces.

4. Take note of how you were able to heal your physical body in this manner. Is there a commotion going on? Were you aware of the presence of a hostile entity, or did you manage to return safely with the assistance of a guide? If you can maintain track of all of these in the future, you'll be able to keep track of your future projections and how to channel them in order to make them more efficient, which will be really advantageous. A logbook is not necessary to be kept indefinitely. Once you've gotten used to it, you might wish to jot down some quick observations. Remember to cease practicing fully; you'll be able to do so more quickly because you'll already know what time, place, and other factors will be most conducive to your achievement at that moment.

Take Control of Your Environment

You can also improve your influence over your environment by employing some of the tactics described below to gain more control over your astral projections:

- **Manage the level of noise in your home:** are there any other sources of noise in your home besides your alarm? Do you have a grandfather's clock that goes off every day at midnight? What kind of noise does your air conditioner (or any other electrical equipment that you use on a regular basis) make? Take a minute to examine whether it would cause harm to a third party, regardless of how accustomed you have become to it. Instead of employing a computer system that produces interference, project your photos using a fan. If your windows are rattling, make sure they're properly sealed to prevent future problems. Make a note of everything that could interfere with your sleep or cause you to lose focus that has to be addressed ahead of time. Consider and plan for all of these scenarios ahead of time.

- **Prepare your friends and family:** the people in your immediate surroundings may be big sources of dispute, which you should be aware of before beginning to project. Is there someone in your family that calls you every day at the same time? Is it feasible that your flatmate may knock on your door at dinnertime to inquire about special orders? Is it more frequent for your partner to cuddle you without your permission in the middle of the night? All of these are things to consider ahead of time in order to manage your estimates properly. Reduce visibility by closing your shades or properly sealing your door, and, if possible, notify people that they will not be able to stop you at certain hours of the day.

- **Don't forget to look after your pets:** if you sleep with your favorite dog curled up next to you, your body may struggle to adjust to getting out of bed without him. Other astrologically connected entities, in addition to dogs, may cause them to respond. If this occurs, keep your pets away from the projected projection area. Keep them out of that area and lock your door to keep them out and away from your things.

Remote Viewing

Remote viewing is a basic psychic ability. It is the concept of seeing something that physically is not present. Though remote viewing can be accomplished with or without the use of an object or place as a marker in time and space, it may also be accomplished by pure clairvoyance. This ability is what makes remote viewing unique from clairvoyance, psychometry, and even precognition. Sometimes it's referred to as objectless remote viewing because no object needs to be present at the time of viewing. Remote viewing can also be described as prospective remote viewing to differentiate its' usage from past remote viewing (i.e., flashbacks, past life experiences). Some have described remote viewing as psychokinesis, but this is not true. Psychokinesis is the ability to directly manipulate physical objects through the mind (i.e., bending spoons). Remote viewing does not fit under that category because it does not involve any physical manipulation of matter or energy.

Remote viewing allows you to see what's happening in a location that's either Earth-based or in intergalactic space if you are capable of having a simultaneous out-of-body experience (OBE) while remote viewing. It has been used to identify enemy targets in the Gulf War, locate planes that have gone missing, and even locate kidnapped victims. The US Military claims that remote viewing was used in Desert Storm with positive results.

Students of remote viewing learn through demonstration and practice and study many of the techniques that are used by clairvoyants and psychics in general. Remote viewing is a decision-making skill where you learn to view an object in time and space and then analyze and interpret the images that your mind creates. You also learn to work with a team or individually.

Psychic art is an individualistic pursuit; however, there are different ways that remote viewing can be accomplished. The first way requires two individuals—one the target or subject, the other the viewer. The second method requires one person—you! This method allows you to both be your own subject and viewer at the same time, thus eliminating any possible confusion. This method is called objectless remote viewing.

Remote viewing is a natural part of who we are as humans. Even the most skeptical people on earth have had an experience of remote viewing at some point in their life. Examples include déjà vu, dreaming, or "The Twilight Zone." These experiences could be remote viewing related. It's a normal occurrence! The ability to do objectless remote viewing requires tremendous amounts of training and discipline to accomplish; although, it's one of the least understood psychic abilities. Objectless remote viewers are few and far between due to the time and effort required to learn it properly.

Remote viewing is a form of clairvoyance, though it does not require an object. It has to do with seeing what's happening as if you were physically there. To do this, the viewer projects themselves both mentally and psychically to the remote location where the object or event is taking place—or to the target at which they wish to focus. Oftentimes, the target used for training purposes is a picture, chart, or map of some sort. This object becomes like a roadmap for them when they go into their consciousness to remote view. Though many remote viewers have used this method to achieve their goals, it should be noted that objectless remote viewing is possible.

Conclusion

Empaths are extremely sensitive people who have a remarkable capability to perceive what others are feeling and thinking among them. They are born with the capability to comprehend the individuals they come into contact with on a deep level. They are aware of the basic motives, goals, and desires of others. In a way, they are able to connect with other people and thoroughly comprehend them on such an emotional level, whether knowingly or unconsciously. Simultaneously, empathetic individuals unconsciously acquire other people's emotions and sensations.

Empaths face many challenges as a result of their capacity to strongly connect with others and adopt their energies. This seems to be particularly true if the empath is unaware of their intrinsic capacity and/or is accompanied by very toxic as well as manipulative individuals. People who are empaths, for example, suffer greatly from incomprehensible bodily, psychological, as well as emotional suffering. They might get exhausted from chronic illness, stressed out, but also pressured by their heightened sensitivity. To conclude, empathic persons are very sensitive to the emotions and feelings of others. As a result, people (often unintentionally) absorb other people's energy and have a difficult time dealing with external factors.

Psychic abilities come in a variety of types. Some individuals have the ability to see into the future. Some get signals from the afterlife.

Few people can interpret other people's thoughts or sense "auras" that indicate how they are feeling. If everyone possesses some underlying psychic ability, developing yours may be a measure of various sorts of self-awareness. Meditation is among the most effective strategies to develop psychic powers since it helps us to access our subconscious and all of that lies there.

Empathy is a very effective technique. It may assist you in trusting your gut and opening your heart toward others. However, if you're an empathic person, you are aware that there can be a drawback. No one is flawless, and that is a fact. Don't become so concerned with the concept of self-defense that you overlook to live a happy life. People always have imperfections, and this is what makes us human.

If you notice yourself receiving the negative effects of someone else, shielding is a sort of self-care that may be highly useful. Shielding is really about defending yourself while also enabling your mind to rebalance, making you feel easier and much more in your emotional control. Empaths are very sensitive people who are acutely aware of others' feelings and intents. In reality, they get so focused on others that they neglect to look after their own needs. This scenario arises, at least to some extent, from a wish to avoid upsetting other people's emotions.

To be an empath is a blessing, but it may sometimes seem like a burden when you're feeling stressed. If you think you're an empath, use self-care strategies like those listed above to safeguard your energies. If you exercise them on a regular basis, you may notice that your abilities continue to get better as your confidence grows.

Made in the USA
Columbia, SC
26 September 2023